I'm rarely interested in talking about myself. I prefer to listen. What follows is a selection of what I heard over the course of a thousand trips as an Uber driver. These stories are non-fiction, which is to say they happened in real life.

There are two types of Uber passengers: the mute and the talkative. The talkative can be further divided into the ramblers, who are pure gold, and the inquisitive. The inquisitive passengers ask one or two of four standard questions. These questions are boilerplate, as if on a checklist, so I fell into boilerplate answers that would either require people to engage in more interesting conversation or indicate to them that they might consider shutting the fuck up.

Just once I would have liked somebody to ask "So, when was the last time you did something stupid?" or "You wanna hear about how I made our waitress watch while I licked my boyfriend's eyeball at an Indian restaurant?" or some similar gem. Nope. Everyone asks the same four questions, so I gave everyone the same answers.

Q: So how long have you been driving for Uber?
A: Either "about four hours" or "about a year" depending on how much I wanted to avoid small talk.

Q: So where are you from?
A: Either "Texas" or "the moon". If the latter, I would ask if they'd ever been, then launch into a soliloquy about how it's such a pain to live on Earth with all the gravity and the traffic lights.

Q: So what brought you to [this city]?
A: Either "my kids are here" or "I'm on the run from the law". Once in a while people asked what I did to become a fugitive. Once in a while I made something up.

Q: So what else do you do besides this?
A: "I do so many things..."

With the exception of the last story, identifying names and places have been withheld to protect the innocent and the guilty alike.

John Puckett
Charlotte, North Carolina 2018

SOMETIMES WHAT'S LEFT OUT IS MORE FASCINATING THAN WHAT'S PUT IN.
OR, WHEN THE TITLE IS AS LONG AS THE STORY.
Female, aged 25-35
Pickup location, U-Haul lot

"You live in a quintessential neighborhood," I said.

"Yes, it's very tranquil and domestic-looking," she replied.

"Oh, that's the perfect cover for you."

"You're right," she said.

TRANSPORTING MINORS ACROSS THE STATE LINE
Children, aged 5-10
Pickup location, strip mall parking lot

The name of the passenger said [Sean]. When I got there I saw the guy waving me down was six-foot-four, three hundred pounds, so when I got out to open the door I said "What's up Big Sean."

If you don't know, Big Sean is a hip-hop artist currently in heavy rotation. This guy knew, because he chuckled and said "Sup, player," as he gave me a clap-and-snap handshake. "Ay, I'ma have you take my kids to they momma's house." He assessed my nonverbal reply carefully. "Cool. 'Preciate you. Hang on hang on." He then took a phone call while I made sure his kids got buckled in the back seat.

They were two boys, probably three years apart. Little private school uniforms, giant bookbags weighing them down, shy and quiet, but very polite. They were each carrying a bag of takeout food.

"Did you guys have a fun day at school?"

"Yes sir," the big brother said.

"Have you got a little snack there? You can eat it in the car if you're hungry."

"We got spaghetti."

"Oh, probably don't eat that in the car," I said.

"No sir. This is our dinner."

Big Sean came around to my window, leaned down and said "Be careful. They precious cargo."
I told him don't worry, I'd treat them like my own.
He told the kids he loved them and to behave themselves, they said yes sir, and we departed.

I've driven children before. It's probably a violation of Uber's policy but guess who doesn't care.

One kid I drove had an appointment at his headshrinker's and mom was held up at work so she called an Uber so he wouldn't miss it. He seemed like a pretty sharp kid. He told me all about his little league team and how he just moved here from D.C. because kids were bringing drugs and guns to his school (he was eleven) so mom and dad decided to head for greener pastures. Another kid was on his way to soccer practice with mom when her car broke down. I arrived at the same time as the tow truck. She told him to go with me while she went with the tow truck and she'd pick him up after practice. He did not want to get in my car alone. He pleaded for mom to come with us but she was harried, so first I had to put mom at ease. He watched that exchange and felt a little more comfortable.

I'm sometimes stunned by the level of trust people place in a complete stranger to handle their children, but when the stranger is me I think nothing of it. I have two kids. I know how kids are, how they behave, what they need.

Big Sean's kids were delightful. I asked if they had lots of homework, they said yes sir. I asked if they liked their teachers, they said yes sir. They didn't feel much like chatting, I could tell. Sometimes when kids get out of school they're invigorated and sometimes they're exhausted. These two were exhausted.

When we got on the highway I turned on some classical music. Five minutes later I glanced back and they were both sound asleep. They napped for thirty minutes.

When we got to mom's neighborhood I turned down the volume on Franz Liszt and said "Almost home boys." The older brother woke up and looked around, recognized where he was, and gently shook the little brother's shoulder.

When we parked in mom's driveway I got out and held their spaghetti while they hoisted their bookbags onto their shoulders.

When they filed up to the front door I waited to make sure they got inside safely.

When the door closed with them inside, I got back in the car and left.

THIS IS WHERE THE FUN STARTS. AND THIS IS WHERE IT STOPS.
Female, aged 30-40
Pickup location, lakeside mansion

I pulled into the circular driveway of a giant house on the edge of [Lake Welch] late one night to pick up a guy named [Steve]. When the door of the house opened a woman stepped out in a dress and high heels holding a tidy handbag and looking every bit like she was ready for a night on the town, but it was already two in the morning.

She stopped and turned to look at the open door behind her, through which a man with white hair and a white bathrobe came scurrying, barefoot and smiling. He put his arms around her waist and kissed her neck while she stood still, letting him. They exchanged a few words I couldn't hear, he kissed her on the cheek, she let him do that too, then she turned and walked to the car while he lingered in the open doorway.

Uber suggests you always ask the passenger's name to confirm you're picking up the correct person, so when she got in the back seat I asked "Are you Steve?"

She chuckled and said "No, I'm [Julie]. That's [Steve] there, like a puppy watching me leave."

"How was it?" I asked.

"Oh, it was nice. We went out to dinner at [Stella's]." The kitchen at [Stella's] closes at ten but she refrained from describing what they'd done in the interim four hours, leaving it to my imagination. "So, John. Where are you from?" she asked.

It's often jarring and not unpleasant when someone uses your name. I was surprised she even knew mine. "I'm from Ohio," I said. "How did you know my name?"

"I'm not going to get in a car this late with a complete stranger," she said. "A girl can never be too careful."

"That's true. Although knowing my name is hardly keeping you safe."

"That's also true. But it's a start. Plus I always carry protection."

"Do you."

"Of course. You know what I mean, don't you John?"

"Of course," I said. What's your flavor?"

"Glock, forty caliber."

"Very nice. Simple, just point and shoot," I said. "The forty has a kick though, doesn't it."

"Yes, that's entirely the point."

[Julie] was not to be trifled with. She spoke in a low, even tone. Plenty of inflection but controlled, pleasant but firm. She sounded like she'd done this a zillion times, giving men the impression that trying any monkey business would be ill-advised. I certainly wouldn't have tried anything, though I did consider several propositions.

Her phone rang.

Hello… Yes, all finished… It was fine. Standard… Well I'm on my way home, so… It's three hundred an hour… Ok, let me know.

I asked what kind of work she did. She said she was a welder, an artist who made sculptures out of metal. She showed me photos of some of her work and of her studio, a garage on the edge of the ghetto where rent was still reasonable. It was easy to imagine her in grimy overalls and a welder's mask, focused on creating.

When we got to her neighborhood one of the roads was closed, so she helped me navigate a detour.

"This will take us back around to my house, past the country club. Have you been there John?"

"To your house or the country club?" She chuckled. "Yeah I've been there a few times, but just in the driveway. That's high society. I wouldn't know how to conduct myself."

"I'm sure that's not true John."

"Do you keep saying my name to make sure you have my attention?" I asked her.

"Oh I know I have your attention."

"You sure do."

"That's my house on the right, the one with all the lights on."

"That's sweet, someone left the lights on for you."

"Yeah, me," she said, exasperated.

"Aw, there's nobody to leave the lights on for you?"

"No. But i'm fine living by myself. I can leave my dirty towels on the bathroom floor all I want."

"Tsk tsk [Julie]. First chink in the armor there."

"Oh, letting you know I live alone," she said as we pulled into the driveway. The house was a picture of domesticity with potted flowers, a new Range

Rover in the driveway, and a small fluffy dog in the window waiting for mommy's return. "I know you're not a threat John."

"Oh thanks, that's nice of you to say," I replied as I put the gearshift in park.

"Besides, I have a Mossberg pump-action shotgun in the house. And i'm a light sleeper."

I laughed and said "Noted."

"Thank you for the ride," she said as she opened the door and got out.

"My pleasure Steve," I said and she chuckled. "Sleep well."

She walked in the front door and closed it behind her, then the lights went off.

THE FUN SIDE OF COMMERCIAL INSURANCE
Male, aged 30-40
Pickup Location, airport

If I pick people up at the airport it's never from the queue. I only get the request when the request levels are so ridiculous that Uber abandons the queue altogether and takes any car available that's even remotely close to the airport. Then I avoid the Arrivals area. The line of cars waiting to pick people up is a quarter mile long and moves at a glacial pace, until you reach the curbside pickup at which point it becomes a frantic jockeying for space, where cranky, tired travelers await. No thank you.

I got smart the second time I picked up someone at the airport. I called him and asked if he'd be willing to walk upstairs to Departures. I said we could be out in thirty seconds, versus the bedlam going on where he was. He agreed, but seemed put out.

I said to walk upstairs and stand under the sign that says American Airlines. He said ok. Five minutes later I drove right past the long line of cars waiting for Arrivals and right up to the curb at Departures. It was empty. No cars, two or three smokers piddling around, and two security guards normally there to direct traffic, but there was no traffic, so they were just chatting with each other. It was as calm and quiet as a _____. My passenger was nowhere in sight. I parked under the sign that says

American Airlines. He wasn't there. Nobody was there. I looked up and down the sidewalk. Empty. So I called him again.

"Are you at Departures?" I asked. He said yes and sounded perturbed. "I'm under the sign that says American Airlines but I don't see you anywhere. I don't see anyone actually."

He said "Well I'm here, and this is turning into a real hassle".

Just then one of the traffic cops came up to me and said "You can't park here buddy" and I said "I'm picking someone up, he'll be here in thirty seconds." and the cop said "Where is he?" and we both looked up and down the concourse to see it devoid of people. I said into the phone "[Jim], the cop is telling me I have to leave. If you're not here in thirty seconds I'm going to have to drive around again."

[Jim] was now audibly aggravated. The cop said to me again "Come on pal, just drive around." And then I was audibly aggravated. "[Jim]," I said, "I'm sorry but the cop is telling me i have to drive around. Do you see the sign that says American Airlines?"

"I went to Departures like you told me to," Jim said.

"Ok, look up and tell me what sign you're standing under."

As I'm waiting for his response I drive past a giant black SUV with tinted windows, the only other car within three hundred yards, parked all the way at the end of the concourse and shielding from the world's view a man looking up and around at the signs above his head. I stop the car and yell out the passenger window, "[Jim]?". The sign he's standing under says Lufthansa.

He gets in.

"You know I travel to this airport all the time and I've never had such a difficult time getting picked up," he said.

"Well you did a great job of hiding behind that SUV. How often do you come here?"

"Two or three times a year for the past eight years. It's never been this hard. This is just ridiculous."

"You here for work?" I asked.

"No. I just want to get home and go to bed," he said and with that he put on a set of headphones. He was about sixty years old, white hair, polo shirt with the logo of some country club in Florida. I judged him to be an entitled rich old white man, possibly illiterate, definitely tired and cranky.

The third time at the airport I picked up Dan. Dan wasn't like that at all. Dan's his real name. He said I could use it. He suggested in fact that I use Dan Dan the Insurance Man but that's too much to type every time I need to indicate him speaking.

I was four miles from the airport when I got the request. That means heavy traffic. I called on my way.

"Dan, this is your Uber driver."

"What's up man?"

"Arrivals is a mess right now. If you want to walk upstairs to Departures I can get you home fifteen minutes quicker."

"Yeah, great! I was gonna say the same thing."

"Good," I said, "I'll be there in five minutes."

"Ok. I'm wearing a blue shirt and black pants, and I'm at the valet stand at the far end."

I already loved this guy.

I zipped up to Departures and spotted him immediately, tall, fit, and smiling. When I got out to put his bag in the trunk we shook hands and he said "Thanks for picking me up up here. I do this all the time and I always call the driver and ask if he'll meet me at Departures. Downstairs is always a fucking nightmare."

"Thanks for being an awesome person Dan," I said and he got in (front seat) and we were off. "How was your flight?"

"Uneventful. Which is exactly how you want a flight to be," he said. "No screaming kids, no hijackers, no delays, just over an hour up and down. I didn't get seated next to a hot girl but at least the guy next to me wasn't fat or snoring, so there's that."

"Nice. Do you fly a lot for work?" I asked.

"Yup."

"What kind of work do you do?"

"Commercial insurance," he said.

"Oh." I listen to corporate drones talk about work all day long and I don't know how some of these people don't kill themselves. The jargon, the politics, obsequious underlings and faux-humble bosses. It's the worst. I'd survive exactly ninety seconds in that environment before being fired for telling the truth in ordinary English. "Please don't start talking about that," I said. He laughed.

"Yeah, it's real fun at parties when someone asks me what I do. It's like an off switch. I say commercial insurance and people start checking their watches." I laughed. I found it difficult to imagine how a bright, talkative guy like this could bore people at a party.

"Maybe your job title is putting people to sleep."

"Yeah, it totally does but it's just like the easiest shortest description. When people ask *What do you do?* they usually just want to know how you make money. So i just say commercial insurance and they're like *Oh that sounds interesting* while they're eyeing the exits. By all means, please fuck off. I didn't want to talk to you in the first place," he said. I was cracking up.

"Is it fun?" I asked.

"Yeah, it is. I get the businesses that the big firms won't even take their calls they're so ridiculous, so I see a lot of crazy shit. Like you know the [Ten Hands Brewery] over on [Hartsell Blvd.]?

"Yeah, I take people there all the time. Invariably some IPA lover with a beard and suspenders."

"Exactly. So the guys that own the brewery want to have axe throwing."

"What?"

"Axe throwing. You ever see those lumberjack competitions on tv where they throw an axe at a sideways tree stump with a target painted on it? LIke darts, but bigger and way more dangerous."

"You're joking," I said. I could not contain my giddiness.

"Dead serious."

"So they want people to come and drink beer and throw axes."

"Yes."

"Well that fits with the lumberjack-chic clientele," I said.

"Yeah. They don't understand why their insurance quote is so high. They're like *Damn dude that's expensive* and I'm like well, it's kind of a high-risk venture."

I was now laughing uncontrollably. "Dan, commercial insurance sounds like the funnest business ever."

"Yeah, it's pretty fun. I mean I don't have to wear a suit for this kind of shit, so I'm just drinking a beer in jeans and a t-shirt at three on a Wednesday, talking to these guys while they show me their plans for a bar-slash-trauma factory. " I considered asking if he needed an apprentice.

"Dude, you should say all that instead of 'commercial insurance'."

"Oh I do sometimes. What do you do besides this?"

"Bartender. Just like you, when I say I'm a bartender people form their own impression of me based on what they know about that job in general. So sometimes I don't let people do that. I *give* them the impression I want them to have. So they'll say *What do you do?* and I'll say I relax people and they're like *Oooh, how do you do that…* then I say stuff like oh, you know, I administer a quantity of alcohol, a little food, if someone needs to talk I make them talk, if they need silence I give them that, and all of a sudden people are like *Um, where do I sign up*. Any bar in the universe."

"That's awesome," Dan said. "Yeah when I tell people what I actually do all day they're interested. You know Lloyd's of London?"

"Of course," I said. "They'll insure anything."

"Yeah, totally. I have contracts with them so I go to London occasionally and sometimes a girl will hear that and she'll be like *Ooooh London?* and I'm like I was invisible until you found out I wear a suit, please go away."

"Is Lloyd's going to write the policy for the drunken hatchet fest?" I asked.

"They'll write it but I don't think these guys can afford it. One of the guys was like *Let us shop this around* and I was like ok man, good luck."

EARNERS AND CARETAKERS
Male, aged 25-35
Pickup location, brewpub

I get to the pickup location but can't drive into the parking lot because a large BMW is leaving and doing a swell job of blocking the entrance. I'm on the street trying to turn right, the BMW is turning right out onto the street but doing so from the wrong side of the exit, making it impossible for me to squeeze in. The man driving the BMW is old. White hair, stooped posture, slightly confused countenance. The woman in the passenger seat looks like Donatella Versace, also old but with a kind of frail glamour, long yellow hair, giant black sunglasses, big lips. I'm able to notice all this while I'm waiting for them to get the hell out of my way, which they do finally. My passenger is standing in front of the building watching me. He gets in.

"That was nice of them to block the entrance like that," he says. He's a big man, maybe six-three, two hundred fifty pounds, with a full beard and a voice that's low in register but slow and friendly.

"Yeah, you saw that huh?"

"Yeah," he says, "they've been here for three hours. I was watching them at the bar. They seemed kind of weird. The lady was like sixty five years old but she was behaving like a teenager. I think she may have been European."

"Maybe it's a Russian-bride type of deal," I say.

"Yeah, maybe he ordered her on the internet."

"It happens."

It's three in the afternoon. He'd been at the pub since noon and he's on his way to another microbrewery, but he doesn't sound or smell drunk. "Did you have lunch?"

"Yeah," he says, "I had grilled chicken. It was pretty good. Not as good as mine though. I'm slow roasting a seven pound pork shoulder for dinner tonight. I give it a rub with salt, pepper, paprika, brown sugar, a few other things, let it cook all day."

"Sounds delicious. Are you a chef?"

"No, I just like to cook. I got these two hand-held shredders made specifically for pulling apart barbecue. They're basically claws. You hold them in your fists like Wolverine and just go to town. They're awesome."

"Are you having a party? Seven pounds of pork seems like a lot, how many people does that feed?" I asked.

"Nope, no party. That's just the way we eat. I keep an eye on meat prices and I buy when I get a good deal. I got a seven pound pork shoulder for thirteen bucks."

"So you're just having a few beers while your pork shoulder cooks?"

"Yup," he replies, "I usually drink beer on Wednesdays."

"Why Wednesdays?" I asked. I was expecting him to say Wednesday is his day off work.

"On Wednesdays the three breweries around here run specials, three dollars for any pint. One brewery specializes in sours, one makes traditional standards, and one makes weird experimental shit like lemon-basil-saison and oyster porters and stuff like that."

"Sweet."

"Yeah. My wife said I could day-drink on two conditions: if I don't come home blind drunk and if I don't drive, and I was like Honey you got a deal, so I just have a couple of beers at each brewery and I take Ubers."

"And a delicious, economical dinner will be ready when she gets home from work. Sounds like you two have a nice system worked out."

"We do. We take care of each other."

"That's nice," I said. "I just dropped off a girl who said the same thing. She was on break from working a double. She was going home to feed her dog and her boyfriend. She said 'If I don't give him food he won't eat.' and I said 'The dog or the boyfriend?' and she said the boyfriend. She said the dog will eventually get into the cabinets or tear open his bag of dog food or something, but the boyfriend is a computer programmer so he sits in front of the screen with his headphones on for hours and hours and he just forgets to eat. I was like 'Yeah sometimes dogs are smarter than boyfriends.' and she said 'That's usually the case. But I love him. We take care of each other.'"

SAINT BRITTANY
Female, aged 20-30
Pickup location, restaurant parking lot

It's ten at night on a Thursday. I pull into the parking lot of an Outback Steakhouse. Usually when I pick up people at restaurants they're waiting by the front door or at the valet stand. Not [Brittany]. [Brittany] is pacing in small circles in the middle of the parking lot, preoccupied, one hand with her phone to her ear, one hand dangling a carryout bag and a big purse draped over her shoulder. The weather is nice so I have the windows down and I can hear her side of the conversation.

"Baby... Just tell me where you are and we'll come get you... No!... No... Baby are you serious? I was just bullshitting with him, it's totally fine. He was fine with it... Yes... Just tell me where you are and I'll bring you your steak and shrimp... Yes, don't you want it? You hardly ate anything. I want you to have it... Baby..."

She pulls the phone away from her ear and looks at the screen, drops her hand to her side and sighs. She opens the front door and gets in next to me.

"Sorry," she says, "my boyfriend and I got in a fight." She is magazine-cover good looking, no makeup, plain clothes, but outstandingly feminine, an angel with a carryout bag full of warm protein on her lap. I can't imagine anyone wanting to fight her. "Would you mind just driving around the block," she asks sort of worried and sort of weary. "He couldn't have gone far."

"No problem," I say. And it's not a problem. It's the literal opposite of a problem. As an Uber driver driving around the block is the whole point. Whatever people need, if it involves driving around, you do it. I've driven escorts, drug dealers, car salesmen, preachers, drunks, the old, the infirmed, newlyweds, children, a professional mermaid once. Everyone's got someplace to be. [Brittany's] got no place to be. She just wants to drive around the block. "Not in a hurry?"

"Kind of. I have to work tonight." It's already ten-fifteen at night. My guess, she's a nurse working third shift.

"Oh, ok. Let's find this guy then," I say. We begin driving around the block. "What are you fighting about?"

"Nothing. It's his birthday so I took him out to dinner. We were sitting at the bar and the bartender didn't know how to make a royal flush. And this other guy sitting at the bar was like, I know how to make a royal flush, it's ten through ace all the same suite, which was cheesy, but I just wanted the drink. So I'm like you want me to jump back there and do it for you? and the bartender was like relax I'll make you one, just tell me what's in it. And then my boyfriend got all bent out of shape because he thought I was being rude. He said I was being obnoxious, but I wasn't. Everybody was having fun except him."

At this point her phone rings. *"Baby... Yes, I'm sorry... Where are you, will you please let me come pick you up? What are you talking about... Baby, how are you going to get home?... Ok."*

"He's back at the restaurant. He said this is the last time."

"The last time that what?" I ask.

"I don't know."

We arrive back in the restaurant parking lot and her boyfriend walks over to the car. She gets out and they both start to get in the back seat. Before the doors even close the boyfriend is saying "This is the last time you embarrass me like that [Brittany]. I'm sick of it. This is the last time. I've had enough. I can't handle this bullshit anymore. This is bullshit. I thought you loved me. Bullshit."

"Baby, ok. I do love you. Please calm down." Brittany says. Her voice is calm and imploring.

"Take me back to my apartment and collect all your shit and get out of my life. I'm done with you."

"Baby, are you serious? Can we just talk about this tomorrow please. I have to go to work in-"

"I'm done with your bullshit."

He is manic, irrational, not listening to a word she's saying. He continues to berate her on the way to his apartment, she continues to try to soothe him. People argue in the back of the car sometimes but this is uneven and difficult to listen to.

We park in front of his apartment building, a sleek new highrise on the edge of downtown. "Don't bother getting out. I don't want you in my apartment. Ever again. We're done. Just stay away from me." I wonder how she's going to collect her things without going inside.

Brittany says "Ok. Will you please take your steak and shrimp? You haven't eaten anything-" Under duress and she's still thinking of his well-being.

"I don't want it. I don't want anything from you," he says, "Just leave. I don't want to see you ever again." He gets out and slams the door and stomps toward the building, then turns around and marches back, so she opens the door for him, but he doesn't get in. He leans in and says "Can I have that canister?"

"Of course," she says, and fishes through her purse to find it. She hands him a little film canister and says "Will you take your food too, please? You haven't-"

"I don't want anything from you." He slams the door in her face and stomps into the building.

I'm not sure what to do. She lets out a sigh and says "Alright, I guess just take me home. I'll pick up my stuff tomorrow."

"That guy has some issues," I say.

"He's under a lot of stress. His contract at work is expiring and he hasn't found a new job yet." I can't believe she's defending him after the way he treated her. There must be no bottom to her well of caring. Definitely a nurse, I think. We pull away from the curb. Now her phone rings again.

"Yes… Well I don't know what to do, I have to go to work... You said you didn't want… Can we please just talk about this tomorrow… Are you serious? Baby, please…"

"He said I can't believe you're just going to drive away."

"But he told you to leave." I say, confused. This guy is driving me crazy and I'm not even dating him.

"He said he's going to put all my stuff on the sidewalk."

"He says come collect your stuff then he says don't come in my apartment ever again. He says he doesn't want anything from you then he says he wants that canister. He says get out of my life then he says I can't believe you're leaving. You seem like a nice person, why are you putting up with this shit?"

"I don't know," she says, "we just have a chemistry. That fire and ice, you know?"

I wonder who is which, who's going to melt, who's going to be doused. "Is he really gonna dump your stuff on the sidewalk?"

"I don't know."

"Do you want to go back and look?"

"Yeah. I guess I should."

We drive around the block. Back in front of his building, we see a pile of belongings.

"Well. I guess that answers that." she says. I get out to help her transfer everything into the car. It's warm out and quiet on the sidewalk.

"So are you homeless now?" I ask as we're putting bags in the trunk.

"Oh, no. My apartment's over on [Hawthorne]. The [Blendon Building]. I was just staying at his place to watch his dog while he's at work all day." Helpful. Every time she opens her mouth she gets nicer and nicer. Her tone is equanimous even in the midst of this turmoil. She seems like a woman who's learned to handle life's tribulations with aplomb. I admire her composure. We finish loading the car and she gets back in the front seat. "Thanks for helping me. This probably isn't what you want to be doing right now."

"You're a paying customer. I'll do whatever you need."

"Thanks."

"What time do you have to be at work?" I ask knowing the [Blendon Building] is ten minutes away, and we'll have to unload all her stuff.

"Around eleven."

"Are you going to be late?"

"No, I'm fine. As long as I get there around eleven." she says.

"What kind of work do you do?"

"I'm a dancer at [The Platinum Club]."

"You're a stripper?"

"Yup."

Ok, I think, *that's kind of nurse-adjacent.*

THREESOME
Male, aged 30-40
Pickup location, leafy old neighborhood

It's midnight on a Wednesday. The good people of the city have gone to sleep. Traffic is nonexistent. A trip that takes sixty minutes during rush hour takes only twelve minutes now. It's gloriously serene. On many streets the trees on each side branch over the center and create canopies. It's like driving through lush tunnels. It is my favorite time to drive around, a lack of business notwithstanding.

I pull into the driveway of a nice home in an old but well kept neighborhood. The house has an illuminated doorway but all the interior lights are off. I idle, wondering if anyone is home, if I'm at the correct destination. Finally, a man comes halfway out the door carrying a twelve pack of beer, checks his pockets, sets the beer down, goes back in the house, reemerges minutes later, snatches up the beer, walks briskly to the car, opens the rear door and gets in and says "Sorry, I forgot my weed."

"No problem," I tell him, he's my last ride of the night so I'm not raring to get on to the next fare, plus I'm sympathetic to the forgetfulness that attends pot smokers.

Some passengers are chatty, some are mute. Some will try to engage in conversation to be polite the way you might with a lone stranger in an elevator if you knew the elevator ride was going to take eleven minutes. This guy's a talker. The destination is close by, but in the short span I learn much.

He just got back from Dublin, he was there all summer. Mom and dad are at a beach resort in Uruguay and he's staying in their house while they're away. He doesn't really work. He drove for Uber last year during the golf tournament, just to see what it was like. Man you pick up some crazy people, don't you? He had three guys offer him an extra hundred in cash to find them some girls, like he was some kind of pimp. They were up from Dallas for the tournament, executives from the sponsoring bank who got special privileges, clubhouse passes, two of the guys were father and son and they got to play the course during the pro-am. The father was like that's the way a real golf course plays and junior was like yeah it makes our country club look like the ghetto. Two snotty fucks and a douche-in-training is how he labelled them. He was going to visit his friend from high school. They went to a Catholic high school together and kind of lost touch after graduation but he tries to stop over and hang out with her whenever he's in town. She's super cool, single mom, works her ass off with no help. They were the oddballs in high school and they've been friends twenty years since.

We have difficulty finding her apartment. It's an enormous complex spread out over a half-mile and all the buildings look the same.. He calls her and she tries to guide us in but we are rats in a maze. As he's talking to her on the phone I'm staring at the navigation, trying to get as close to the pin as possible. He says "She says she sees us." We drive around a corner and lo there's a woman dawdling in the parking lot who waves at our headlights. I pull up so the car's bumper is inches from her knees. She smiles and does not flinch or move aside. He declares unnecessarily "We found her." He thanks me for the ride and asks "You wanna come in and have a beer and hang out?"

It's late summer. It's late at night, dark and quiet. There is no temperature and no breeze. The day is over, I am finished driving people around, and I can think of no reason not to oblige.

"Yes. Yes I do. Thanks." I turn the Uber app off for the night and leave the car where it sits, not bothering to park it. There is nobody astir to notice or care. As a substitute for my name which he doesn't know, my passenger introduces me to his friend as the coolest Uber driver ever. She offers her hand which I shake.

He gives us both a beer and small talk ensues as we ease our way to her apartment's front porch.

We sit. She tells us to speak quietly so as not to wake up her son sleeping inside. My former passenger (now he's just a guy I'm hanging out with- let's call him Phil) fishes out his weed but he has no bowl in which to smoke it. His friend says she has one inside but again, we must be quiet lest her son wake up.

We take our beers inside.

In the kitchen, Phil continues to talk at a normal volume level. His friend continues to shush him while searching for the required utensil without turning the light on. It's a small apartment, not tidy but not messy. I could see how everything came to be where it is. A blanket hanging off the couch, some papers on the table, a few dishes in the sink, a translucent orange-red scarf draped over the lamp glowing in the living room.

The kitchen is small and we are close to each other.

She checks drawers and cabinets and finally finds what she's looking for. I excuse myself to pee. From the bathroom I can hear Phil's voice clearly, despite her protests. He is quiet only while the implement is in his mouth but then goes right back to jabbering. When I return from the bathroom she says we're going to her room where we can shut the door. I was just in a different room with the door shut and I could hear Phil easily, so I'm not sure what this will accomplish but I am a guest here and I do not argue.

She leads us into her room.

Once we are all in she shuts the door behind us. The moment the door latches closed, as if by magic, Phil's voice drops to near a whisper. The bed takes up nearly all the floor space. There's a dresser, a closet, a window. Two original paintings hang on the wall. "Did you paint these?" I ask her. She demures. They're engrossing and I stare, mute.

"What are you looking at?" she asks between Phil's hushed sentences.

"They're very good. I can see your brush technique in this one. Playful but disciplined."

She's a talented artist but she doesn't want to hear it. She's embarrassed, so I look around for something else to focus on. On the bed there's a book open, face down. It looks like she was reading it before we came. I flop down and pick it up. It's thick and heavy, like a reference book. It's a book of spells and incantations. "A painter and a witch?" I ask.

"I'm just practicing." she replies.

"Practicing painting or spellbinding?"

With her hand palm-down she describes the perimeter of the bed and says "Do you see any paint here?"

THE THINGS I'LL DO FOR SIX BUCKS
Male, aged 35-45
Pickup location, subdivision

I picked him up in a barren and featureless subdivision, new, so the trees hadn't grown up yet, two hundred houses that all looked the same and sidewalks that connected them but otherwise lead nowhere. Streets a half mile long, every one curved to give the effect of meandering through the countryside but also making it so a terminus was never visible. The standard suburban "neighborhood" where nothing happens but yard work and charred burgers on the back patio, and bedtime. It's safe for kids to ride their bikes in and out of the street but offers them no opportunity to ride to the corner store to pick up a carton of milk or a candy bar. By regulation there are no corner stores, no commercial activity, no chance to interact with strangers and the wider world. In the morning people must wake up and go elsewhere to live their lives- to work, to shop, to see a movie, the bank, the post office- and they come back to their chicken coops to put up for the night.

I had the misfortune to stay in a subdivision once, for four years. Like most subdivisions the prominent design feature of every dwelling was the garage. It's the main entrance, so you can drive right into your house. The front door is rarely used, it's mainly for show. I had a neighbor across the street when I was stuck there whose garage door would open every morning and he'd back his car out, the garage door would shut, and he'd go off to wherever he went all day, then in the evening he'd pull into the driveway, the garage door would go up, he'd drive in, and the garage door would go down. For four years this guy lived eighty feet from me and I never knew his name. I never even saw him out of his car. He may not have had legs for all I know, I only ever saw his head and torso. I think once we might have waved at each other. Point is, isolation often prevails in these places, despite the population.

When he got in the car it had been dark for hours already. Bedtime. The day was over for all but a few whose flickering blue tv screens gave the only indication of "activity". I don't remember much of the dialogue with this man, but the words I do remember I remember verbatim. "What's up man?" I said.

"Hey," he replied. His breathing was labored and full of heavy sighs, as if he were forcing his diaphragm to work properly. It seemed to me he'd been crying. He rubbed his thighs with his hands.

"Getting out of the house for a while?" I asked.

"I don't live here anymore," he said. His voice was shaky and fearful. I wondered if that meant he'd been evicted just then. It would have explained his condition.

"[5513 Glenforth Rd.]?" I inquired of the destination.

"Uh, yeah, sure." He said this like the destination didn't matter, like he chose it at random and didn't care if he actually got there.

The impression that remains is of his mental and emotional state. A state of distress. On the verge of resignation. A man at the end of his rope, ill at ease in the world. He began to piece together sentences, something about his kids and his ex-wife, and how he didn't care anymore, and how he was glad it was over now, or would be soon. He mentioned something about nobody missing him. As we got out of the subdivision he laid down in the back seat and breathed in quick, heaving fits. I became concerned about his physical health.

I'm familiar with such a group of symptoms. I know what interior condition they indicate.

I drove slowly, allowing him time. He wiped his eyes and his nose and sniffled. Then he sat up and took a few deep breaths. At the moment we were approaching a railroad crossing and he said in a mild panic:

"Can you actually stop right here? I'll get out at these train tracks."

And I thought *Nope. Absolutely nope. There's zero chance I'm letting you out of this car near a set of train tracks.*

I held him in the car against his will, which may or may not be kidnapping, I ended the fare so he wouldn't be charged, and I drove around without aim until his agitation subsided.

It took twenty minutes.

He noted in an even tone that we were driving past his church, so I pulled into the parking lot and asked if he was ok.

"I think I will be," he said.

He asked if he could get out and I asked him what he was going to do.

"There's a little graveyard behind this church. I'm just gonna sit there for a while."

I thought that was a fair idea, so I told him to take care of himself and he said thank you. I watched him walk behind the church, then I drove around to where I could see the graveyard and I saw him slump down against a headstone, and I watched.

Twenty minutes more passed.

Finally, he pulled out his phone and made contact with someone. I turned the Uber app back on and drove away, waiting for the next passenger to summon me.

A HALF-DEAD CHEF AND PETULA CLARK
Male, aged 25-35
Pickup location, suburban apartment building

Sometimes people aren't ready.

When you arrive at the pickup location they're still upstairs putting on eyeliner or rearranging their stamp collection or whatever people do. They've requested the ride, they know how long it'll take for the car to get to them, and they're notified when the car arrives. And still they're not ready. It annoyed me when I first started but now I don't mind because it gives me a chance to get out of the car and stretch. I'll usually walk around to the passenger's side so when they come out I can open the door for them. People appreciate that. I'll lean on the car and close my eyes and tilt my face toward the sun while they're inside hitching up their stockings or searching for their passport. Invariably the person comes out and says "Sorry!" to which I reply "Are you apologizing for interrupting my nap?"

I'm leaning against the car, feeling my skin cells manufacture vitamin D. Birds are chirping, leaves rustle mildly, the air smells of cut grass. I could wait like this forever. Inside the car Muddy Waters plays on my iPod, *Well now it's...late on in the evening I feel like... like goin' home.* Eyes closed, I hear a door creak open upstairs. What seems like minutes later I hear it latch shut. I do not look. If it's my passenger I'll know in a few seconds.

Another minute passes and nobody has approached, so I open my eyes and look toward the building.

A guy in a chef's jacket is standing at the top of the staircase, gripping the railing with both hands, head hanging. *Woke up this mornin', all I had was gone.* It looks like he's fortifying himself for the first journey, down the stairs. I watch. Without raising his head he takes one deep breath, releases one hand from the railing, and puts one unsteady foot on the step below. Pause. He makes the next step down, then the next, so slowly I go back to sunbathing. Delta blues, indolent, play like a soundtrack while he descends, *Minutes seem like hours and hours… gonna seem like days.*

Finally at the bottom of the steps, he asks "Are you my driver?"

"Yep." I say without opening my eyes. He does not move. I turn to appraise him. "You ready?"

"Yeah."

He shuffles over and I open the door for him and he says thanks. Alcohol emanates from his pores. He smells like an emptied glass of bourbon. He pours himself onto the seat, comes to rest in a position that makes it appear as if he has no bones, a puddle.

We pull out onto the street. "Rough night?" I say.

"Last night was great. It's this sunshine that's killing me." Sunlight slants across his neck and chest. He spreads open his jacket, presumably so it can hit closer, kill him faster.

In order to turn on to the main road we wait behind a few cars, which puts us squarely atop what I know to be a disused railway line. "You want to just sit here on the train tracks for a while, see what happens?" I ask him.

He looks left down the tracks, then right. He sees the cars in front have moved forward but we do not move forward with them, we stay on the tracks. He lolls his head back onto the headrest and closes his eyes. "Yeah. That'd be fine with me." he says, resigned, maybe praying for death. We remain, though I know death is not coming. At least not by rail. Biffy Clyro now on the iPod, *I'm never gonna sleep again... I get to do it all wrong.* It's a raucous and hopeful tune but I sense he's not ready for this either, so I turn the volume way down.

"You gotta work the lunch shift?" I ask.

"Yeah."

"We should probably get going then." He gives no reply and I don't wait for one. I proceed off the tracks and on to the main road.

"You have good taste in music," he says, "This is one of my favorite songs." He's alive, barely. "Normally I'd say turn it up, but…"

Lately it's hard to let you know… that I'll never learn.

"No problem," I say, "you don't want to rock out. I've been there."

"I mean sometimes I need to howl like an animal," he says along with the song, "and last night I did. Literally. It felt good." *I got the rage, I always got the rage.*

"I've been there too." I say. "I have just the song for you."

"For me?"

"Yeah. Something to get you ready for your shift, pump you up. Get you in the right frame of mind. You know how when you're cooking through the rush and you forget what time it is and what day it is and where you were last week and whether you paid the electric bill, and you're crushing it, and you forget that you even have a body, much less that it's hungover, and you're putting out plates in rapid succession, every order perfect, the expo calling for food and you telling him two minutes now please shut the fuck up, and the expo saying you kiss your

mother with that mouth? and you saying no but I
kissed your mother with it and the other line cooks
fuckin' howl and the expo laughs and the
waitresses are running your perfect plates out fast
and hot and you're just killing it and for a split
second you think to yourself, this life ain't bad at
all?" *I am explosive and volatile, I'm on the turn.*

"Fuck yeah I do." he says in a low grumble, eyes
still shut, head still laid back. He's fully alive in
there now, but still hurting.

"I've got just the song for that."

I scroll through the iPod to find the hardest rocking
song in there, but I see something better, and I
push play.

*When you're alone and life is making you lonely
you can always go...*

He laughs from his belly and sings aloud,
"Downtown!"

SOMEONE LIKE YOU
Female, aged 40-50
Pickup location, suburban office building

I get the request and recognize the pickup location.
It's the corporate headquarters of an automotive
company. I pick up and drop off salespeople there
all the time, they all plod up to the manor house to
make their pitches. Some of them come bounding
out, some trudge. The parking lot and the two
major streets surrounding this building are under
construction and it's a pain in the ass getting in and
out of there. I've done it dozens of times, so I
know. As I'm pulling in, the passenger calls me.
(Which is always annoying, by the way. I can't see
the navigation if I'm talking on the phone, so calling
me to give directions sometimes causes me to go
the wrong way, the exact opposite results you're
looking for as a passenger.)

"Hi this is [Lori] I'm your Uber passenger?"

"Hi [Lori]. What's happ-"

"So the building I'm at is surrounded by
construction so the best way for you to get in here
is to turn down [Coltrane Street] and come in
through the parking garage. I'm standing at the
entrance to the parking garage so when you get in
here go through the parking garage toward the front
door and I'll be standing right in front of the front
door." I'm already in the spot she's directing me to,

so I can see her standing there talking to me on the phone. She's staring off into traffic looking for a sign of my arrival. I'm already walking around the car to open the door. "The construction is really bad so it's kind of a pain to get in here so if you have any trouble-"

"[Lori]. I'm right behind you." She turns around to see me holding the door open for her. She drops the phone from her ear and drops her shoulders. She collects her briefcase and carry-on bag and marches toward the car.

"You would have found me without my help wouldn't you," she says.

"I appreciate your desire to help though. That's very nice of you."

"Sorry, it's habit. Not everyone thinks it's so nice."

The destination is the airport, so I say "You going to the train station?"

"No, the airport. Does it say the train station? I thought I put in the right destination but sometimes the navigation is weird."

"No, that was a joke. Nobody ever goes to the train station. Ever."

"Ok good. I usually go right out of here and take [Braden St.] to [Hanover St.] and then [Hanover] all the way across town. You could take [Braden] to [Wendell] but I don't know what the traffic is like at this time of day. It's rush hour so I'm not sure which way is quicker. I guess I'll let you handle that."

"Sure. Why don't you take a little nap. It's twenty five minutes to the airport, you've got time."

"Pssh, nap. I have a ton of emails to reply to so I'm just gonna sit back here and do that. The more I get out of the way now, the less I'll have to do when I get home tonight."

"How many?"

"Um…" She scrolls through her phone. "A hundred and forty six."

"A hundred and forty six emails? That's a lot. You know you wouldn't have to reply to them if you just deleted them." She lets out a surprised laugh.

"Oh no, that would not be good."

"Yeah. That's what everybody says."

"Well, it's part of my job."

"Of course. Alright, you answer your emails, I'll drive the car."

We make it past the construction onto [Braden St.]. The windows are up, it's quiet in the car. I hear her phone make a noise like the sound of a fighter jet launching from an aircraft carrier. A miniature electronic roar. A minute goes by and I hear it again. And again. And again. I hear the sound of a plane taking off six times in the span of five minutes. "Is that the sound your phone makes when you send off an email?"

"Yeah."

"It's very satisfying! I can see why you'd want to do it a hundred and forty six times."

"Yeah," she says, wistful, "It's the little things."

We make it down [Braden] to [Hanover] but I go east on [Hanover] instead of west. Airplanes continue to launch from the back seat. After another half dozen takeoffs she looks up to see where we are. "Oh did the navigation tell us to go this way?"

"Well it told me to go this way. You weren't really involved in the decision."

"Oh."

"That probably drives you nuts, doesn't it."

"I've just never gone this way before."

We proceed in silence. Planes are no longer roaring off the deck. She's looking around in every direction. It's hard to tell if she's nervous or aggravated or both. I don't tolerate uncomfortable silences well so I say "Lori."

"Yes?"

"You're right, the shortest, most direct route to the airport is west on [Hanover], but it's a surface street and there are dozens of stoplights between here and there and every one of them gets backed up at this time of day. We'd wait for the same stop light twice, at least, the whole way there. A seven mile trip takes an hour. It's quicker to go out to the highway and shoot all the way across the city."

"Oh. Ok," she replies.

Placated, the fighter jets resume their sorties. The trip takes just under twenty five minutes. As we pull on to the airport access road I ask her what time her flight leaves. She says not for another hour and a half.

"Perfect," I say, "you'll have time to send the other hundred emails and have a bloody mary at the bar. Then you can relax on the flight."

"Yeah, right," she says. It seems like the notion of relaxing is foreign to her. I wonder what she's like when she's unfocused, unencumbered, when she's finished being busy. I know lots of people like her. "I won't be able to relax until I'm in bed."

"Oh, is that when it happens?" I ask, knowing it probably doesn't happen then either.

"Actually no. I lay there thinking about all the stuff I have to get done the next day. My only hope is to work myself to exhaustion every day so by bedtime I'm ready to just crash out."

"Well you're doing a great job of it today," I offer in earnest.

"Thanks," she says.

The sound of real planes taking off punctuates our parting.

WATCH YOUR MOUTH
Male & Female, aged 30-40
Pickup location: [The Coliseum]

A concert had just let out downtown, at [The Coliseum] which holds twenty thousand people. It's a bit of a nightmare negotiating the center of the city when this is happening. There are people and cars swarming over every street and side street, people darting into taxis, cars streaming out of parking garages, drunk pedestrians spilling off the sidewalks, horns honking, police yelling, a general low-level pandemonium. If you were sitting on a bench watching it'd be entertaining. When you're behind the wheel it's stressful. Uber's surge pricing makes it an attractive proposition but I've found it's not worth the extra few bucks, so I avoid downtown when this is happening. On this occasion I had just dropped someone off down there and was, inadvertently, in the center of the commotion.

When I got the request I was two blocks away from the pickup location, on the same street, two stoplights between us. Ordinarily this would take ninety seconds, but I had to wait for the first stoplight three times, such was the traffic. I was progressing by inches. As a courtesy I called the passenger with a status update, and to try to smooth out the pickup.

"Hi [Andy], this is your Uber driver. Traffic is a mess but I'll be there in a few minutes. Can you tell me where you are, exactly?"

"Hi. We're outside [The Coliseum]."

There are ten thousand people outside [The Coliseum].

"Um. Ok," I said, "can you be a little more specific?"

"Uh, we're in the median on [4th Street]. If you drive down here we can jump right in."

"Good," I said. "When I get there I'll have my flashers on and headlights off so you can spot the car easily."

"Ok, sounds good."

I was still waiting at the second stoplight, for the fourth time. I couldn't move until the cars in front of me turned left, which they couldn't do until there was a break in traffic, which there wasn't because the other ten thousand people were trying to drive in the opposite direction. I waited for the second stoplight six times.

Eventually I made it through the light and halfway down [4th Street] where the median was and, naturally, there were three hundred people standing waiting to get into cars or cross the street or catch the trolley. I turned my headlights off and flashers on as promised, and drove slowly, slowly enough that I began to feel the psychic weight of the very long line of cars behind me. I was scanning the crowd frantically, waiting for someone to wave me down. Nothing. No indication that my passengers had seen me blinkering and holding up traffic. I cruised by at a walking pace, conspicuous, giving every opportunity to be spotted. Nothing.

I travelled past the median and was headed for the next red light, with several cars in front of me and several hundred cars behind me. Window down, I heard someone yelling "Hey!" and looked in my side-view mirror to see a man running after me.

"Hey are you our driver?" he asked as he got into the backseat without waiting for a response.

"Are you [Andy]?"

"Yeah."

"Then yes," I replied.

"My girlfriend is back there," he says sheepishly. "Do you think you could turn around?"

I thought this was the breaking point. She couldn't have been more than fifty feet back, why didn't she just run up here with him? Now he was asking me to do a u-turn, in the middle of the street, in the midst of the heaviest traffic the city ever sees, to go back fifty feet and back toward the congested morass that had sapped my patience.

"Are you fucking kidding me?" I blurted. Just then the light turned green. To drive around the block to pick her up would have taken half an hour. To sit there at a green light to wait for her would have brought the wrath of dozens of impatient motorists behind me. I was insane with frustration and paralyzed with indecision.

Suddenly, mercifully, a taxi going the opposite direction stopped in the middle of the street to let in passengers, blocking the flow of oncoming traffic and allowing space for me to whip the car around, which I did with haste.

The car wasn't even straightened out in the lane before a woman walked across the street with her hand out. I put the flashers on and got as close to the curb as possible. Through my open window I addressed her: "You must be the girlfriend."

"No," she replied, curt, as she got into the back seat next to [Andy].

[Andy] said "Oh. She's my friend, and she's a girl. I didn't mean my girlfriend." I didn't care. I was just relieved they were both in the car and we could be on our way.

Then the girl friend says, in a nasty tone, "What took you so long. And why didn't you see us."

This was the real breaking point. I recognized God was testing me and I knew I would fail, if my pulse rate was anything to judge by. It didn't seem she had any idea whatsoever what was going on in the city around her. They both sat silent, waiting for my reply.

Now, what I might have said was: "Well let me tell you what took so long…" But what I actually said was: "I'm not talking to you." like I was eight years old. Truth was, I was afraid of what might come out of my mouth. I have a tendency to say the wrong things, which in this case would have been *You are a monumentally self-absorbed bitch*. I figured keeping my mouth shut was the best option.

It wasn't.

Because I channeled the stress and anger I was feeling into the foot that controls the gas and brake pedals, and the three of us almost died on a highway exit ramp that night.

THE GIMP STORYTELLER
Male, aged 30-35
Pickup location: orthopedic clinic

I pull up to the front of an orthop
young man with shaggy hair, glasses, a
steps out of the glass doors. He's wearing a black
trenchcoat and hobbling very slowly using a cane.
His right leg is immobilized with a brace. I roll down
the window and ask if I can help him into the car.

"No, I don't need any help, thank you. All I need is
time."

This becomes obvious as it takes him a solid sixty
seconds to open the door, bend into the passenger
seat, and hoist his leg gingerly in. He sits in the
front seat, which is rare. Most people sit in the
back like a taxi or a limo.

I check the destination and confirm, "You headed to
the library?"

"Yes," he says.

"What's happening there?"

"On Wednesdays I read stories to children."

"Very cool," I say. "Is it fun?"

Yes, it's fun. Children have no problem suspending their disbelief. They're a receptive audience." I ponder this for a moment and think of my own children and conclude this is a fact. Mr. Trenchcoat stares through the windshield. "I like your hula girl."

I have a little plastic hula girl shimmying on my dashboard. It's not kitschy or ironic. I put it there because my daughter gave it to me as a gift and I want her to see that I use and appreciate it. "Thanks," I reply, "My kid gave it to me for Christmas. She was walking through the dollar store and it caught her attention. *That's it! That's what daddy needs!* she said. Turns out it is exactly what I need. Everyone loves it. It's for sale if you're interested."

"How much?"

"A million dollars," I say in all seriousness.

"Hmmm," Mr. Trenchcoat says as if considering the proposition. "If you're gonna get a million dollars for it you need to come up with a better story. Something which demonstrates a more... exclusive provenance."

"Oh yeah?" I say, humoring him, "What kind of story would you tell about it?"

"Maybe it used to belong to Jim Morrison. It was gathered in his personal effects by his agent or his girlfriend where it sat for years, until a private auction was held. It was bought by Prince, who kept it on his kitchen windowsill. When Prince died it was stolen by one of his housekeepers as a memento. Given all the treasures Prince owned, the housekeeper justified the theft by telling herself nobody would miss this little piece of plastic. What the housekeeper couldn't have known was that Prince's will specifically stipulated that the hula girl be donated to the Rock N Roll Hall of Fame. When the executors of his estate went looking for it, it was gone, so they started asking questions. The housekeeper, fearing discovery, implored her cousin to take it for safekeeping. The cousin, a thug with no appreciation for art and barely any conscience, showed it to you and told you the whole story while riding home from the meeting with the housekeeper. Fortunately for you, he was drunk and alas, dropped the hula girl on the floor in the back seat of this very car and forgot about it as he spilled out at his destination. Something like that."

"Wow," I say, "that's a great story." I don't think it's believable, but for producing it on the fly Mr. Trenchcoat showed talent.

He shifts in his seat and grimaces, repositioning his leg this way and that way. He looks uncomfortable. I don't want to mention it and force him to focus on his discomfort, but it doesn't appear that random conversation is distracting him from the pain either, so I think I'll give him some non-physical space to stretch out. Maybe if he talked about it it would hurt less. "So what happened to your leg?"

"I got shot."

"What?"

"I got shot. Usually I tell people it was crushed in a car accident so I don't have to tell the real story, but that's not the truth."

"Who shot you?" I ask, stunned.

"I actually don't know. He was wearing a mask."

"A mask? Are you serious?"

"Yeah. When I was younger I used to get into a little bit of trouble. Nothing too serious. I was part of a group called The Green City Underground. We operated around town for three years or so. You know what a flash mob is? It was kind of like that but we would pull elaborate pranks. It took a lot of planning for these things and since I have good organizational skills I was usually the one to map everything out, coordinate materials, task assignments, timelines, exit strategies, stuff like that. Nobody knew each other's real names for purposes of plausible deniability. They called me

The Professor. The few times we were caught I used an alias. If you look up the police reports from around that time you'll see a few arrests of a guy named Nate Goodman for trespassing, disturbing the peace, vandalism. That was me. It was the most generic name I could think of without it sounding made up. Anyway, we were just a bunch of disaffected youth. Frustrated kids with lots of angst and energy and few outlets. But due to the anonymity and the blatant disregard for the law, we attracted some unsavory characters. Genuine criminals. My roommate at the time was a guy everyone called Tacitus. I mean that wasn't the name on the lease or anything. He wasn't on the lease. He was just a guy I knew from the Underground who crashed on my couch most nights. He paid me a share of the rent every week, in cash. I later learned- the hard way-" as he says this he massages his right thigh, "that he earned his money by selling drugs. Strictly small-time. An eighth here, a quarter there. But he had this girlfriend whose parents lived in [Briggs Park], upper crust, country club, poodle, BMW. Privileged suburbanite who relished telling her prep school friends she was going out with a drug dealer. Compared to their lives he was a real gangster. A bad boy. Well of course word got around that this so-called drug dealer was staying at my place, and one night some guys came looking for drugs and cash. At the time I was living in a gated apartment complex with an intercom system. They pushed the code for my apartment- which leads me to believe the girlfriend was complicit somehow- and said they were here to see Tacitus, who was on the back deck smoking a cigarette. I didn't think anything of it since there were always Underground people coming and going. They knocked on the door and next thing I know I'm sitting on the couch with a gun pointed at me while two other guys start tossing the place. Tacitus slides the back door open and comes in and the gunman swings his piece around and points it at him. His hands go up immediately. And he pissed himself. He was visibly trembling. 'Where's the money.' the gunmen asks him. Tacitus can't produce a word. 'Where's the fucking money dude.' he asks again. I could tell he was just as nervous as Tacitus. Probably his first armed robbery. His voice was excited and the gun was shaking a little. I didn't want anybody getting shot even by accident so I started to say 'Hey man, calm down, let's just-' but all I got out was 'Hey man', at which point the gunman swung his piece back around toward me and as he did it went off. You don't put your finger on the trigger until you're ready to pull it, especially if your finger's shaky. Everybody knows that. Well guess who didn't know that. Fucking amateur. The bullet went through my knee and up into my thigh. Caused all kinds of damage to bone and muscle. It hurts every day."

"Wow," is all I can say.

We park at the library door and he begins his struggle to get out of the car.

"Time to do it for the kids," he says. "Thank you."

Those kids are lucky I think.

AN ARTICULATE CAT
Female, aged 35-45
Pickup location, suburban neighborhood

It's a warm evening, the sun is on its way down having done its job for the day. It's that time when people have made it home from work, changed their clothes, made their calls, they've fed and walked the dog, and they're ready to get out of the house and get on their own schedule. They've put the workday behind them and they're excited to relax and socialize. I like being a brief part of this transitional phase between drone and free person. They're always full of anticipation as I shuttle them away from drudgery toward *bon temps*. Today is Tuesday.

I park in the middle of a cul-de-sac not knowing which of the five houses my passenger will exit. I get out and lean against the passenger's side of the car. Soon a woman comes down one of the driveways, unhurried, big smile on her face, texting on her phone while she walks toward the car. She's dressed for a night out. Not fancy but done up.

"Congratulations for going out on a Tuesday," I say.

"I know, thanks! Friday nights are for the bridge-and-tunnel crowd."

I'm surprised she used that phrase and peg her as a transplanted New Yorker. I open the door for her and she gets in the back seat.

"[Blackbelle Pub]?"

"Yeah," she says, "I'm meeting my girlfriends for dinner. How's your day been?"

"So far so good," I say. "The [Blackbelle's] just around the corner right?"

"Yup."

"Yeah, I've given rides there or back a few times," I say. "All the right people eat there. It's the hot spot."

She laughs. "Oh yeah, I'm high society," she says, sarcastic. "I'm a regular Daisy Buchanan." I'm surprised again by the reference. "Have you ever eaten there?"

"Oh no. I'm not properly credentialed," I say in mock deference.

She affects a swank British accent and says "Oh you simply must try it. The fried cheese curds are exquisite."

"Oooh, fried cheese curds?"

"Yeah," she says, "the food there's really good. It's kind of a meat market but I always agree to go 'cause it's so yummy. My girlfriends eat the olives in their martinis for dinner and flirt with every handsome smile in the room while I'm crushing a bacon bleu cheese burger and sweet potato fries in the corner of the booth like an animal."

"Sounds delicious."

"It's so good. Do you live in [Fairview]?" she asks.

"Nope. I live in a magical little village called [Williamsville]." I say, doing my best to put lipstick on a pig.

The small town I live in is awful. There are no hot spots. There isn't even a coffee shop. When I first moved there I asked the girl who cut my hair So where do people go to get coffee here? and she said What do you mean go get it, you make it, in your kitchen. And I said No, like when you're out running errands and you need some caffeine and to sit down for fifteen minutes? and she said Well, the Shell gas station has the best coffee in town.

The Shell gas station.

The town's a thirty-minute drive from anyplace. The median age of the population is old. Obesity is the norm. I'm not judging, just stating the facts. The only social activities seem to be going to church and blocking the aisle at Walmart. It's boring. If you want a slow pace and peace and quiet it might be the best place on earth. But I can only handle so much peace and quiet before I start to go a little crazy. Spending too much time there is stupefying.

"Oh, I used to live in [Williamsville]!" she exclaims.

"Are you serious?" I ask, incredulous. This woman is attractive, literate, engaging, exactly the kind of person you'd expect to meet in a big city, and the kind I've never met nor would ever expect to meet in an armpit like [Williamsville]. "Almost nobody lives there. Most people don't even know where it is."

"I know. It's the worst," she says.

"What were you doing there?"

"Absolutely nothing. I used to be married to a guy whose family owns the [Ogden Millworks], the big factory out on [Highway 15]?"

"Sure, I know where that is."

"Yeah. It drove me crazy. Like literally insane."

"I know the feeling," I say.

"Yeah. My ex-husband and his family were super traditional and they didn't think it was appropriate for a wife to work, so I sat at home all day, every day. You know there's no place to go there. I had nothing to do."

"Right."

"So I got a cat, to keep me company. And then I started talking to the cat."

"Everyone talks to their pets."

"No, I would have whole conversations with the cat, all day. It was my only outlet. I'd ask the cat's opinion on politics or religion or fashion and then I'd make up the cat's responses. I'd answer myself in a different voice, as the cat. Like if you just had an audio recording of any given day it would sound like I had two different personalities."

"Well I'm sure the cat was articulate."

"Oh yeah, smartest cat in town for sure," she says, smiling. "I would put it on a leash and take it for walks."

"You walked your cat on a leash?"

"Yup."

"Ok, that's crazy."

"I know! I was so bored."

"Well you seem pretty well put together now," I say as we arrive at the valet stand. "It must have been temporary insanity. Congratulations on your recovery."

"Thanks," she says. "Good luck up there."

FINANCIAL CRIMES
Female, aged 30-35
Pickup location: bank building, downtown

"Hi, how are you?"

"Ugh, I'm better now that I'm out. Please get me away from here as fast as possible."

"You're going to the Renaissance hotel?"

"Yes please."

"Are you just getting out of work now? It's nine thirty at night."

"Yes."

I often pick up young professionals late at night from large banks and I always ask the same question and usually get the same reply, which is *I don't know* or *I hope so*: "Is it worth it?"

"No. It's not," she says without hesitation. "They treat us like indentured servants. I feel sorry for the people who have kids. Their kids are texting them *Daddy are you coming home for dinner* or *Mommy are you coming to my recital?* but they can't leave. They have to make a good impression. This is actually an early night for me. Usually I'm not finished until ten or eleven. I left early but only because I'm taking work home."

"Home? You live at the Renaissance hotel?"

"I do during the week. I'm from New York. They fly me here on Monday and I stay through Thursday then fly back."

"Every week?"

"Yes. It's getting very tedious. I want to run away to one of those Caribbean islands and live in a little beach shack."

"Yeah, everyone wants that but nobody wants to do what it takes to get it."

"I know. I mean why do I need to buy two hundred dollar shoes? Because everyone else is wearing them. I'd be fine with twenty dollar shoes but they would notice."

"So?"

"So you have to fit in, speak a certain language, wear certain clothes. It's part of the corporate culture. I'm sick of it. I'm sick of thinking about financial crimes."

"You mean you're sick of thinking about how to prevent financial crimes?"

"No," she laughed, "how to present data in a way that's unlikely to draw attention from regulators."

"Oh. So you help cover up financial crimes."

"Well. That's a matter of perspective."

"Is it difficult?"

"It takes some effort. The hardest thing to get used to is how casual people are about big numbers. For example, there was a matter of one point five million dollars that could not be accounted for. We didn't know where it went. It was just missing. A million and a half dollars is a lot of money for anyone. But we have one point seven trillion dollars on our balance sheet. One point seven *trillion*, ok? So we can't find one point five million, but relative to our balance sheet that's totally insignificant. My boss was like 'that's barely a rounding error. Just ignore it.' We were told to de-prioritize it, it simply wasn't important. Someone may have stolen it, we don't know. But nobody cares. When I first started, this sort of thing was incomprehensible to me. Now I think like they do."

"I bet you could make a fortune if you could find all this money, take a percentage of what you recover? You'd have that Caribbean beach shack in no time."

"They don't want to find it." she said, certain.

"Yeah, that makes sense. It's probably already in the Caribbean someplace."

THE HAPPY ENDING
Female, aged 20-25
Pickup location, day spa

High noon, my first ride of the day. The sun shimmers on [Lake Welch] as I drive over a bridge to the pickup location. I pull up to the front of a popular lakeside eatery rumored to be mob-owned, but I see my rider standing a few doors down in front of a day spa.

She's young and tall, shorts and tank top, flip-flops, blonde hair pulled back in a ponytail. She's a vision standing there in the sun. She looks back and forth between her phone and my car, checking to make sure I'm the designated driver. Assured, she opens the front door and gets in and says hi.

"Good morning," I say. She is radiant, and smells faintly of lotion, bright and fresh. "Are we going to [Morehouse Rd. Plaza]?" She fills the car with such lightness and what the kids call good vibes that I hope the three-mile trip takes fifteen hours.

"Yeah, I'm going to the nail salon."

"Oh, what are you getting ready for?"

"If I'm gonna be wearing flip-flops I need to take care of these toes."

"Thanks for sitting up front," I say, "almost nobody does that."

"Oh I didn't know how it works. This is my first Uber ride." She's sitting up straight with her hands in her lap, smiling, like a child.

"Your first one ever?"

"Yeah. I just moved here from [Shelbyville]."

"Down out of the hills into the big city huh?"

She giggles. "Yup. That's for sure."

"Uber is basically phone-a-friend. When you don't have anyone else to come pick you up."

"Yeah! I don't know anyone here. Do you live here in [Henderson]?"

"No. I live way out in the country."

"Oh." she says. She seems disappointed, which makes me feel good.

She tilts her face toward the sun and closes her eyes, still smiling. I watch the traffic. We drive in silence for a couple of minutes. At a stoplight she says "This weather makes me happy."

"It does?"

"Yes. I love the sun. I'm like a bird, when it gets cold I'm going south."

I picture her gliding bodily over the lake, over the city, south over the countryside, down the coastline.

We pull into the parking lot of a strip mall and I scan the signs. The nail parlor is between a sushi bar and a pet store. "There it is." I say and she begins leafing through her purse. "Alright duchess. You got a massage, you're getting your nails done, when you're finished you can go next door and get sushi, perfectly relaxing day."

She laughed. "Yes! Except I don't like sushi."

"Well. They also have vodka."

She laughs again. "Yes. That does sound perfect."

She pauses, hands me a twenty dollar tip on a three dollar ride and tells *me* thank you.

AN UBER RIDE THROUGH THE RIOTS

I don't own a tv. I listen to my iPod in the car, not the radio. I don't have time to stare at my phone. I rarely know what's going on in the world.
Apparently another black guy got shot by the cops. I didn't find out until the day after. And even then, inadvertently. One of my passengers was talking on her phone as she got in the car.

"Yes, we're ok. Yes, mama, we're fine. Yeah, I heard about what was going on at that... Yeah, right at that Walmart. So I called Shaun and told him don't come home your normal way from work, please, and he was like I know, don't worry honey I'll be safe. Yeah... I know. But it was ok. Everybody's fine."

Naturally I asked what was going on near that Walmart. She told me about the cops shooting somebody and about riots and lootings. I had no idea. I'd been driving all over the city all day and hadn't seen a thing.

I saw the Uber heat map glowing red around Uptown at 3:40pm. A shade early for rush hour I thought, but not evacuation-level. It'd be nice to get some of that surge pricing. Of course, I'm out in Matthews stuck in traffic with a kid who normally rides the bus two hours each way to work.

"Yeah, my grandma didn't want me riding the bus to work today." he said.

Why not? I asked him.

"You know, with everything going on…"

I told him I'd been all over the city and hadn't seen anything going on. At all.

"Well she just wanted me to be safe." he said, which I could understand.

I try to make my way into Uptown. I get as close as Myers Park, where I pick up a lady who's meeting her husband out for dinner.

"Yeah, Park Road Plaza. We were gonna go Uptown but that's not happening now, obviously." she said.

It wasn't obvious to me. So I asked what was going on that they didn't want to go Uptown.

"Don't you have a tv?"

Nope.

"Do you have a radio?" She asked the second time kind of snotty, like how could you be so clueless. I told her I didn't know what people were saying on tv or the radio but I could see with my own eyes there was nothing happening around town. "Well just be careful tonight." she offered.

I wasn't the slightest bit worried. I shuttled people back to their hotels from the corporate steak houses in South Park. Nothing. I picked up a couple in Barclay Downs and took them to the airport. They were exploring Charlotte on a layover and even they knew more than I did. "We just heard there are riots Uptown, wherever that is. Stay away from Uptown."

I head directly Uptown.

I get a request from a guy at the Hilton Doubletree in the middle of what everyone keeps saying is bedlam. His shift as a front desk agent now over, he's heading home. "I usually take the bus," he says, "but I decided not to tonight. Thank God you were here. You're the only Uber driver anywhere near Uptown." I'm astonished. Normally there are thirty of us in a square mile. I drop him off in what most people would refer to as the ghetto. Nothing.

I turn off the Uber app. It's now ten at night and I've been driving for nine hours and I'm hungry. A little food truck at the corner of Trade and Tryon sells the best lamb and rice in the city, plus, according to the media, that's where all the action is and I want to see it.

The cops have Trade and Tryon cordoned off so I can't drive right up to the corner. I don't care. Parking spots are plentiful. I find one a block away. It's a nice night and it'll be a nice walk. Some of the people I pass scurry by with their heads down but the majority are in a mood almost festive. They smile and say hi. They laugh. They seem excited. Residents stand on the sidewalks in front of their apartment buildings with beers, spectating and chatting.

Cops are everywhere. The Epicenter is surrounded and there appears to be a crowd, but I hear no screaming, no shots, no explosions, so I look for the food truck. It's not on the corner where it usually is. Of course.

I ask a cop nearby if she knows where the lamb and rice guy is. She's bewildered. "I don't know" she says, looking around like she had no idea who the lamb and rice guy is. She must not work this beat regularly because all the downtown beat cops know the lamb and rice guy, his food is good. I ask if anyplace is serving food. Nobody knows. I check Google maps and call a couple of places within walking distance. Nervous managers apologize and cite their concern for the employees' safety. It's a nice thought, but I'm walking around Uptown and there's nothing dangerous happening here with the exception of my rising hunger and a lack of anyone willing to profit from it.

I walk back to my car, annoyed. People are still headed to join the crowd. Helicopters are parked in the wind around the skyscrapers. Midnight Diner is several blocks away from the hooplah so I drive over there hoping. It's closed. Of course.

I have to go out as far as Plaza Midwood before I find a place that's still serving. It's a dull Wednesday night at Whiskey Warehouse. Off-duty cooks and railroad workers stare at their drinks as I eat. The bartender twirls her hair, looks for something to chat about. On tv, news cameras show groups of people stopping cars and raising hell on 277.

"Man it's so crazy right now," the bartender says, "I'm glad I don't have to leave Plaza Midwood."

I tell her I do have to leave. She gives me my check.

"Stay away from 277, it's dangerous." she says, motioning to a news scene on the television showing rioters stopping traffic.

I go down Central to 10th and get right on 277 on my way northward. Didn't see shit.

I must have been in the wrong place.

It wasn't dangerous at all.

But I'm white, so...